THE UNDERSIDE OF BARK

GAETANO ANTHONY AIELLO

The Underside of Bark
First published in Australia
by Gaetano Anthony Aiello 2023

A catalogue record for this
book is available from the
National Library of Australia

ISBN: 978-0-6486347-0-6 (pbk)
ISBN: 978-0-6486347-1-3 (ebk)

Typesetting and design by Publicious Book Publishing
Published with the assistance of Publicious Book Publishing
www.publicious.com.au

In gratitude to my parents, my wife Jane and my children Cameron and Ashley

Acknowledgement

Many thanks to those who have helped me on this journey. Peter Eason, Rob Johnson, Geoff Kemp, Heather Stewart, Michael Roder, and Lesley Wyldbore for their reading and editing of the manuscript. I thank JM Coetzee for the Preface and Geoff again for the Forward.

Preface

"With tenderness and with a true poet's eye, Gaetano Aiello brings the streets and parklands and beaches of his native Adelaide to shimmering, sometimes phantasmagorical life. The title poem, 'The Underside of Bark,' is a meditation - gripping, hallucinatory, profound - on Australian and South Australian identity, a true dreaming."

- JM Coetzee

Foreword

Unsurprisingly, the kernel of this collection is the poem, 'The Underside of Bark'. Its narrator tells us,

My story begins
Before Terra Nullius
Before the black fella
Danced on the cove
Before the fish were painted
On rock.

A primordial figure painted in "vivid red and white" that pries open the bark of a tree and invites the narrator to write on its "soft underbelly", personifies this time before time. The poem is a meditation on our relationship with the land. Crucially, it questions the legitimacy of this relationship, and suggests that before the question can be answered, we must open a conversation with Australia's indigenous people. But the metaphorical underside of bark is not only a meeting place of indigenous and non-indigenous understandings. It is also a spiritual realm that lies at the centre of being, like Buddhist nirvana, or Jung's collective unconscious. Throughout the collection, the poetry takes the reader on transformative journeys that end, and find solace, in a place "where all pools". Key themes like love and loss, the persistence of the past, spiritual longing, recur throughout The Underside of Bark, but the poetry's most striking feature is transformation.

'King William Street', which opens *The Underside of Bark*, uses the extended metaphor of buildings as wedding guests to take us through a confetti of traffic towards the bridal table where the guests sit. In 'Town Hall Clock', "pipe fifty-three" of the Town Hall's organ detaches itself, and in disembodied form leaves the building, moves towards Victoria Square, catches a tram to North Terrace, and after alighting melds with a tree where "Leaves flutter and strike as organ keys". These transformative excursions become more surreal, imaginatively daring, and thematically complex as the collection evolves, with 'Kangaroo Country', 'The Underside of Bark', 'Rard dman', 'Bill', and 'Shells' the most noteworthy examples. And to write of the collection evolving is to recognise that these extraordinarily visual journeys are chapters in a central journey. The Underside of Bark begins in the heart of Adelaide, thence to adjoining streets, northwards to Calvary Hospital, deep into the outback, and finally into the ocean in 'Shells'. This meta-narrative begins with an urge to escape the confinements of persona and work-a-day routine. But answers that are "stuck in grid lock" at the beginning of *The Underside of Bark* finally come to fruition at the end of the collection.

A striking feature of the poet's explorations is the fusion of imagination and nature. Again and again readers are plunged into an exhilarating metamorphosis of idea into natural object or setting. These shifts arrive at a place that both obliterates self and celebrates its authenticity. Exactly what this realm is remains undefined. It is the "mystery" that Bill builds roads into. A path "without beginning or end". A melody "Older than genetic memory". The water from which "all gardens grow". Ultimately, it is the Shaman's eye of 'The Underside of Bark' and 'Shells', a higher consciousness redolent of love that finds fulfilment in anonymity:

> Perhaps I am the web stuck between gate posts
> In parkland where the moon seals the night.

At times, Aiello hints at an afterlife, or a ghostly presence that "whispers from the other side."

> Leaves on the path
> Are sandals of those
> Who dance in the wind

Sometimes this presence is a shape-shifting personification of a buried past, best seen in 'Tavistock Lane' and 'Rard dman'.

If all of this seems too analytical, I urge readers to just read *The Underside of Bark*. T. S. Eliot noted that we often admire a poem without wholly understanding it. A first reading of The Underside of Bark will take you on fantastic jaunts so compelling that taking the journey will be enough. And with each re-reading the poems give more. What lies at their heart, and the heart of the collection, is optimism and love. A good poem to start with is 'Opening an umbrella'. Concise metaphor creates a light-hearted sense of fun as the narrator "flit(s) down Grenfell Street" carried by his umbrella. This essential delight, this relish in imaginative transmutation, is what makes *The Underside of Bark* so distinctive and enjoyable to read. And the depth of love evoked in poems like 'Calvary' and 'Who lives there' is implicit throughout, as the poet strives for connection with people, places, nature, mystery.

In the best poetry, expression and meaning are indivisible. Language is not used to evoke mentation. Rather, it is transformed and made new by the deep impulses that compel poets to write.

Consider the deft use of structure and repetition to create the brief but intense drama of a footrace in 'The Gift', Aiello's tribute to the Stawell Gift. Or the multi-layered descriptions in 'Shells' that compress the seconds of a near-drowning into a symphony of fevered reverie. As impressive as this collection is in its imaginative reach, it is the precision and freshness of the language that makes the transformations real.

- Geoff Kemp

Contents

King William Street

The gift is in the shifting of shapes
So the street becomes a great table set for a wedding feast
Each building a guest drinking its fill of city workers
As they wait for bride and groom
To waltz down King William Street

The priest wears the face of the town hall clock
The groom's father dresses in marbled grey
Supported from all sides by the long legged
Children who come after him

A black stump of a grandmother
Tiptoes from plaque and cornerstone
For the slightest peek

The gift is in the amber eye
Of traffic light
Which ushers me towards the square

I leave word at each intersection I cross
But my voice is rose petal
In the confetti of traffic moving east and west

The gift is in the faces of city window cleaners
Who dangle down the hair of drunken wedding guests
In the yellow light which is the tablecloth
In the invitation to eat from the bridal table
And by God in the right to set the guest list

Currie Street

On a night so wet cars in their assorted sizes and colours
Are schools of little fish swimming their way out of the city
A truck the size of an Orca presses through white caps
Of the waves of seeing so that tailgate spreads as a fluke
And blowhole on the cabin is the head of a pin
Rising and falling along Currie Street into king tide
As across curved cornea of eye Orca swims by halo
Of the stars along currents mapped by saints
To the eternal feeding ground and after the harvest
Full bellied sleek blackness of dorsal fin slices through
Fathomless breath rising one step above knowing
To chase the herring home

Intersection

There are buildings which prostate towards the sun
Their top floors are tilted heads with sun glass windows
And from their shoulders necklaces flow down
Chests then circle back across facades to necks

Other buildings stare out in meditation
Like cats with eyes prying into the universe
One building with a gaping doorway seems exhausted
A body lying with hip to the ground braced by an elbow
None of them necessarily stare into the other's eyes
And those which sit with legs bent or folded look here and there
All oblivious to the world of ants which stream in convoy

At this intersection where all rests on the foundation stone
Of the General Post Office and gully winds meet
To stir the dry leaves and twigs of discontent
There is a spark at the knees of a long bearded face
Which no one else seems to see as small flames now dance
And in their sway and twirl flick up a leaf of red and yellow
Which rises across the belly and chest of this man
With hands towards the flames

A woman wearing earrings in the shape of trees
With black hair tight as a steel brush
And hammocks of weighted skin under her eyes
And cheeks of dry bark crosses into the intersection

A prince of a man draped in self-belief floats past
As his long mane drapes the back of his shirt painted

With sun flowers and buttoned with pieces from
A Chinese Checkers board

Another walks as if in a kimono with small inching steps
And as her arm moves up a red and blue glow flows
To the ground and holds her gaze until her hand
Flutters like a fan and with pursed lips and closed eyes
She slowly glides towards the lights

In this street where water pools a head rises
Lower lip just above the water line where yellow
Strands of hair run into a blue pool
Eyes a green which draws you inside to where
Pupils hold a reef of stars in their orbit

And me in the reflection so transitory yet here
Small slivers of lapis lazuli necklace my thoughts
And in the authenticity of shedding all that is
I am in the realm where all pools and whether
This is through the power of looking into the eyes of a lover
Or reclaiming the sight of a child to swim in new waters
It means nothing in this gathering of what matters

View From University Footbridge

In their reflection light poles along the river
Stand as oars steadying all question and doubt
In waters cuffed by concrete and held by weir
Where canopy of trees boat sheds closed restaurant
Moored motor craft and silent paths are settled
In a state preserved in glass along a colonnade
To the mouth of King William Street Bridge
Where answer is pillared by light

Practice Fields

If I run point to point from archery field
Down the guts of ovals winged by gums
Across Frome Road to red brick change rooms
By cricket nets where fast balls are faced
In light where moths swarm
While on an oval in centre square
Players huddle in the chase for finals
Then spear towards goal posts
Is my fitness measured in breaths and footsteps
On that long green path through practice fields
Bounded by University Zoo and Cathedral
A catchment of the living domed on a clear night
By a body of stars which runs along a glowing
Path without beginning or end

Opening an Umbrella

As I grasp the handle
Of my umbrella
I sense the stirring
Of the nocturnal
The wings of a giant bat
Wriggle
Black flaps dangle
Cartilage struts straighten
Skin tightens
The frame of my shadow
As I flit down Grenfell Street

Leaves

Leaves on the path
Are the sandals of those
Who dance in the wind

In parkland on my knees
I lace leaves into a wreath
Born from the same soft skin
Of my mother

Town Hall Clock

In the room below the town hall clock
The quartet plays baroque
As above pipes of an organ crane
From their seats in gilded lamp light
I rise as pipe fifty-three
Swing and bend through permanency
Leaving a gap in the rank and file
Of fluted certainty
Lucidity flows into the stalls
Slips into the robes of anonymity
And slides down balustrade of dictionary
Into the street where the full peal
Of this city's bells ring out
And from the face which seals the portico
Tears flow down King William Street
And I run and pick light globes strung
On what might have been washing lines
From end to end in Victoria Square
Each a fruit to nourish a hollow fluted body
Which wants to play a melody
Older than genetic memory
Of a want and right to be beyond arms
Which stretch and mouth from which to speak
Beyond feet which touch the ground
And hold at will the power to skip and play
As one in the rise and fall of the fountains call
Beyond time name and place
But there are cars and buses which circle
And buildings terraced into night

What catches my eye is a tram
And I hitch a ride which slides past
The building with the clock
Now wearing the cap of a cop
I settle with hoodie pulled over head
Until expelled on North Terrace
Into a wash through beds of bronzed
And pedestalled heads
The air thick with jacarandas' spill
Of purple tinsel which drapes a woman
Seated with books at her feet where I rest
Against a tree and ask
"Are you an angel"
Then follows a shortening of breath
The lean into tree
The meld into bark and stretch into branch
The ovation from canopy
As leaves flutter then strike as organ keys

Kangaroo Country

Well into night park bench on a square
Holds for a time the shadow of my feet
In that midlife want and pressing
Towards some sense of place
Moving past the leaves scattered
Over the ground as if sleeping rough
Revealing in their joining the shape
Emblazed on the path of a Kangaroo
Shivering stretching and rising
Questioning every alcove of my parts
Unwinding my trust in certainty
All of me crosses towards this vision
Reaching for the sight
Eternal in transformation

Love is the cardinal point
In the passage towards Kangaroo Country
Giving a bridge across banks of division
Heart breath and pulse
Tail of bitumen carries me up the hill
Squeezing past those who still
Queue across road past public toilets
Under trees and along paths
All of me slides into thigh breast and paw
Reaching for the light
Eternal in transformation

Wellbeing is not an outlier
Even at the furthest square of my reach

Lie stories of survival and relief
Love is the cardinal point
Incredible the twitching
Nose of daylight
Glistens as a slit in the veil of grass
Thrown across a city square
Opens and swallows the night
Nubile the faith baptised in silence
Squeezed from the breath of life
Quickening the pace
Under trees and along paths
All of me plunges into the blending
Receiving the power to lunge and bound
Eternal in transformation

Hopping in a circular motion
In between playground and café
Neck to neck the criss-cross
Division in the landscape
Marked by buses and cars
Along roads through parkland
Right and left the turns
Stitching and threading
Hide to being
Sewing insight drawn from the stars
Quelling all doubt
Under the auspices of tail and hind legs
Accounting to no one for this right
Rising and bounding
Eyes beyond laneways and buildings

Hurrying towards the bus stop
Umbrella in hand
Right at the square
Telling myself not to be late
Lights red where cars have collided
Even the ambulance cannot get through
Stuck here as if everything is predetermined
Questions muscle their way along these roads
Answers stuck in gridlock
Right at the square I ask to join the kangaroo
Extended is the arm of transformation

Veering from street to street
In and out of sight
Casting flight between
The buildings where titles rest
Offending neither pigeon
Ratepayer or council officer
Iridescent particles gather then scatter
Are more than legs pouch and cheek
Squeezed into the skin of kangaroo
Questions I have fall away
Under trees and along paths
As kangaroo feeds
Rightfully in the long grass of names and places
Enshrined on city signs

Tavistock Lane

I press the palm of my hand to bitumen
Against the liquorish black newly laid lane
A neat strip trimmed with no parking signs
Which irons one-way from Amalfi Café
Through where warehouse had stood
To new student apartments
A lane suited up like a cop saying
"Move on there is nothing to see here"
But the lay of this land remains to speak
Surviving the wrecking ball
And I kneel where there is subsidence in the path
Feel laced in black from head to toe
A body no one else seems to see
No one else seems to hear
The tap tap tap from purgatory
Echo through acre after acre of planned streets

Emissaries

What of the emissaries found in the streetscape
All together at least a dozen from their sleeping places
Rising as if a spark has given form and shape
Mine was a gift or a curse to see their faces in the street
Evening towelled the Angel in my sight in yellow light
Molten bronze fused eyes gave way to sight
On twilight when Hercules in the garden
Rightly shouted from across the road
It is time to move the monuments in this town
Act now and slide what they are not from pedestals
Loosen chains crowns and all propriety
So down the street the naked runner came
Running a message from cloisters in town hall
In that moment, the Don hit a six from his crease
Bronzed pigs and cast pigeon danced in the Mall

Wylde Street

Walking down a cul-de-sac which runs to cemetery gates
I pass signs which mark temporary parking zones
Today this street is likened to a conveyer belt
Or chute through which all must pass
Down this street are the eclectic indispensable at their best
Even the street sweeper must know they are part of this
Stopping by the wall he circles and turns back
Towards the city and all those other streets
Right at the point where he returns into the main terrace
Everything about him entering then leaving this street
Everything about this daily task of clearing debris
Toes at the clear water of immortality

In This My January

In the garden of little bridges and walking trails
Of rotundas where proposals are made
Where starburst is more than the name of a flower
And stained glass of hothouse more than window
Where children race along corridors of wisteria
Flicking the little stone of life about
And trunks of bunya pine stand as giant elephant legs
Crushing all inventory
Where the scared lotus flower blooms
And centrepiece of pond is the statue of a child clinging
To the neck of a swan
Here with my back to old tram barns redressed
As research and administration buildings
Offset from the path I circle Parachilna slate
Laid as the wall of a great well where weeping bark huddle
Every now and then in this wall
Stone juts out like a step
Inviting the craning of head into the silent hollow
In this my January what lays before me is the water
From which all gardens grow

North of Those Days

North of those days when we wrestled on the beach
Over which of us would hold a square metre of sand
Right where waterline shadowed our rugby scrum
The highwater mark written on our calves
Halting the game when there was only one
Then the shedding of skin and sand as we shook our towels
Eating hot chips under the jetty
Reading our future in girls sunning nearby
Right or wrong the summers passed
All that is and was and will be
Cast in the pavers which now seal the path
Each a foothold in the streetscape

Wednesday is like any other day
Eat lunch at the coffee shop where the elite meet
Stop by and say hello where they play Sinatra
To those who would enter another pocket of time
To those who talk of wood oven pizza and good wine
Each to their own as we wrestle over football clubs
Righting the score for the umpire's mistakes
Reading our future in our mortgages and superannuation
All that is and was and will be
Cast in the pavers which now seal the path
Each a foot hold in the streetscape

South of my highest watermark
Opens my eyes to revision
Under the blanket of the night to come
The counting of pavers stacked against the shed

High on the list of things to do
The path along the decking into the garden
Eats at my thoughts
Right at the place where terraces meet
Right at the corner I continue my walk
Across the intersection
Comes the call of cockatoos from parkland
East of where I am

East of where I am is where I have to go
As the streets seem empty of traffic
Somehow the parkland spreads like ocean
The blue opens up before me
The waterline rises to my calves
Everything I am swims in these waterways
Rising above my head the high tide
Rinses from me all that I am not
As I come to land
Calf stiffens with a footfall
East of where I was

Self Portrait

In no particular order
The first is the gold wedding ring
The second the glasses which sit on a nose
Slightly bent to the left
The glasses yes there is a second pair just
In case I lose the first in the surf
Like I have done twice before
The nose well that's an old football story
But no one really asks
White hair on my chest
I now wear a cap
Hands have not worked a jackhammer
Or a trowel which might smooth
The wrinkles from my forehead
Or remove the hair where my eyebrows
Almost touch
This is a small inventory of my parts
All this and more
Disrobed and left on the chair of atom
And matter

The Underside of Bark

1

Asleep on a beach
With one arm for a pillow
The other braced against sand
Forearm to palm and fingers
Like driftwood baked in the sun

2

My doze is seaweed
Wicker knitted thin
A basket nest
A headdress
A mask
A hammock
In which to swing

3

The slide into sleep
Is matte-olive today
It feeds on whispers
From the other side

4

Tell you what
If you ever want
To let that print by Possum go
I'll take it off your hands

Only if you tell me the meaning

Conversation turns to the weather

5

On the desk of my dream
Two bundles of pencils
Ranged against each other
Are eager to draw the agenda

6

So in this world of dream
Am I cast as a linear thinker
Moving from one moment to the next
Or Gestalt
More than the sum of my parts

Perhaps some would say
Spaghetti
Or noodled thought

7

One great bowl
From which to divine
The slow-moving river
Through midsummer grassland

A long moving leash
Tied to a little dog sun
As it meanders west

Every once in a while
Sniffing at the clouds
Or pawing at the range

8

A bowl of stars
More than drops of light
More than streetlamps
More than a billion windows
On a billion skyscrapers
They glow
Brighter than the MCG
And ray into the capillaries
Of letters painted on walls

9

Treadmill of light
Along roads
And through cities
Spun from night

10

The shell of me glides
Along tributary into dream

11

Sleep on a beach
Extrudes the sum of my parts
Into the pilgrimage
From five senses
Towards the Shaman's eye

12

My story begins
Before Terra Nullius
Before the Black fella
Danced on the cove
Before the fish were painted
On rock

13

Crater is a gaping mouth
A thin line of shadow
Rims one side
Where a solitary tree bakes in the sun

14

This place
Is more than a snapshot
Of ochre against cave wall

15

Through corrugated heat
Which vibrates in sheets
They come for me
Naked and cross armed
Wrists bound
In a dwindling universe

16

My husk
Is wrapped in possum skin
A meeting of sorts

Where words are said

Did some of you send this young man
To take bark from this tree

The reply
We sent no one
Again the voice
Tell the young man
Not to do so anymore

When people speak of wanting bark
They must send Notice

Voices reply
That is all right
We will do so

17

The sonar ping
Is felt inside me
Through the corrugated heat
Echo ping presses within
Naked and cross armed
Ping upon ping
Wrists bound
Universe so small
An echo ping

18

A figure painted
In vivid red and white
Rises from trunk
A gigantic head
With upper body bending

Hair the colour of summer dusk
Face white and eyes black
Stares grimly through me
Hands and arms outlined in red

This figure hovers near
Stripped to yellow
Where I scribe my presence in the bark

19

What other chance have I
To tell others I was here

And as if reading my mind
Or taking pity on my form
This figure sinks back into the trunk

Hands pry open bark
As if splitting a chest
Leaving open to see
A soft underbelly
The width of a page

20

Will I write of my mother
Combing my hair
Of warriors
The art of war
Will I paint noblewomen
Of Roman descent
Write of myself and others
Holding spears

21

The tucker out here
Is so far between stops
I am not one for nuts and desert mice
I prefer the gleam of forest green

22

And with these words
The ridges rise
And cockatoo light candle bark
All is fern and undergrowth
And my tree of cockatoo and fernery
Is deep within Mc Cubbin's gleam
Of forest brown and green
Of dappled light and shadows lean

23

And what of the tree
A hardened grey figure
Single arm held perpendicular
To the stonewashed bones

Of those who came before me
Crushed by silence

24

Here I come upon eternal witnesses
The light through twitching fern
The earth studded with quartzite
Mountain ash rising from baked earth
The closest shaft of light thin as bamboo
The furthest wishbone and catapult
And in between the glint of bottle green

25

Here for the first time I know the sacred
The timeless void where I shed my bones
They lie embraced on forest floor
The truth of me presses forward
Across valley to opposing ridge
And like a flake of stone from a greater rock
I am restored into all that is
The bark of tree
The conduit within
The dappled light and shadow lean

26

The incessant dot in sonar dark
Cross stitched and hemmed
Between ping in layered dream
Another panel is added to the scene

27

The long leash of the sun
Becomes a culvert
Where shadows run

28

There are those who see
In dots of brailled thought
And those who see in cubes
Silver as sardine cans

29

Those who see through the muse
All tinselled in veil and scarf
All above shackled by triptych
With centre and two opposites

30

It is now with respect I ask may I take bark
From the greatest of the trees

31

And voices speak
This young man who has taken bark
What of this realm will he remark?

Others say
Give him a chance
To be measured in his thought
While others scoff

32

And the head-man says
When he awakes
Let us see if he is more
Than the sum of his parts
More than shadow painted on wall
Let us see if he can converse
With all that lives in the Underside of Bark

If All Is Potential

Because fate or the universe has gifted these letters to me
Chance might have it that as seeds they will reach their full
Potential
And sown into nothingness their tendrils colour the barren
Come see how the stalks climb the opposites staked together
As lattice

Rard Dman

1

In Rundle Street smoke lingers
In cheap midnight speak
Amongst those seated outside the Exeter
At tables concreted to the ground
They strip time like bark and speculate on Rard dman
Debate who adrift has faced
Pisser against walls
Castrated
Beer swiller
Bludger
Rard dman distasteful tester of faith
In the anchored life

2

Rard dman wears the face
Of a barbed wire fence
Dismantled and rolled like a cigarette
Star droppers mesh and all marooned
In a studded field of stone
On the nicotine side of a wall

3

Rard dman reaches in from painted
Transient sign
Burnt peeling whim
Of another time
Last of the line
Has failed to pay the licence fee
And so Pty Ltd decays in flaking rhyme

4

Mullioned strips of light
Frame a plutonian moon
As moth-eaten moss-bitten
Skeletal nuggets of spine pour
Alphabet into being

5

Eddied swirling spine
Swish and swirl
Clank and dank into the drain hole
Of place and time
Rattle tapple dapple
Squelch belch tap tap tap tapple
The tumbling stumbling chromosomes
Pour to the ground in Tavistock Lane

6

Vertebrate speak seeps
From the innards of the word
Fissure thin ooze and gooze
Drips then pools on the street
Then rises and stands as Rard dman
With worms for feet
Periscope tall pissing letters
In shadow against wall

7

Hiss hiss hiss the piss
of Rard dman Rard dman Rard dman

8

Rard dman walks the streets
In a coat hung to his knees
The air about him urine in heat
Drip drip drip swish dapple dapple
Cartilage and bone dazzle dazzle dazzle

9

More than harlequin leaning
Against wall in Synagogue Place
To passers-by who ask for a light
Bus fare home or simply get a fright

10

Before he is shackled by the mob
Before thumb stamps him down
Rard dman melts into pavement
Paint clinging to the sole of an unsuspecting foot
He takes a walk up Pulteney Street
And catches a taxi towards Port Adelaide
Until the taxi driver yells
Hey not in here mate
Get out and find your own way home.

11

Tap tap dapple in the arms of trouble
Here 'The Colac' has stood since 1864
And to prove the point a plaque on a pillar
Like a surveyor's marker reads
Kevin Moon drank here 1924–1994

12

As Buck tied to a cross watches a stripper
Arse and breast segmented by strobe light
All in the ooze and gooze of primal night
A heavy metal band grunts
Some day I'm going to die
And reborn beyond words fly

13

The carpet sticky underfoot
Rard dman takes drink after drink
Quelch and tubble the sink hole bubbles
Until strippers fold like ironing boards
And Buck is stretchered into the night

14

A headache brings light to day
Rard dman finds himself
In parkland by Wylde Street
He lies under canopy
Nestled between shrub and tree

15

Hey you 'right?
Asks a voice from a bearded face
Found you in the grove
And brought you to my camp
What you do there late at night?
Not safe you know

16

He hands Rard dman
A cup of tea and adds
You lost
Stay and grow here like the tree
With bark rooted in the realm of all possibility
An offer to thrive in the actual

17

Ok you want it your way
Then you have three paths
First choice
We go across road
There red brick fence
Live Archbishop
He gives direction
And book to read
Point you path to Heavens door
Right into the arms of the bloke

18

Second we both go across road
But this time we go to Liquor Land
There the grog man
He gives direction up aisle
Where in the doorway the devil's man's leanin'

19

Last
Go to the cemetery
Roll into a grave

Just before they put the dirt in
To cover some other bugger
And it's as if you've never been here
Never painted
Never sung
Never read

20

GeandGoo the voice from the wall
Electrical and Electronic GeandGoo
Radiates night and day GeandGoo

Anguished howl to those who can hear
Remnant calls of the past
Dammed up blood of ancestors
All woven into genetic memory
Nudging alleys with pulse
Dammed up light spills to the anointed few

GeandGoo calls from above broken windowpanes
Over buckled bitumen and parking signs
Over last night's bundled restaurant tablecloths
Down to empty bottles and to the Amalfi coast

21

Mighty GeandGoo calls to Rundle Street
Announces the slobbering Rard dman
Now stumbles along Tavistock Lane
Paints moist palm against downpipe
Tightens his cheeks
Yells *Fuck you all*

Leaps to the brick work three stories tall
Tucks himself into the letters GeandGoo
Debris in the flaking sign
Gerard and Goodman Pty Ltd
Electrical & Electronics

22

Just when you think the streets are settled
In comes the wrecking ball
Elevated above the milling hoard a swing
Cutting things up behind scaffolding

23

Today they came for Rard dman
Righteous jackhammer
Backed by lender and developer
To tear words from the street
Culling sign against wall

24

All is ripple all is speckle all tap tap dapple
Light flickers as dump trucks trundle

25

"No!" Yells out Mighty GeandGoo
Indignant Rard dman Rard dman Rard dman
Pisser of words against wall cries out
"Send in your wrecking ball"

Who Lives Here

The phone rings and no answer as if a back is turned
To the path where shoes once hurdled shadows and skipped
Rope
Where I raised a fist of flowers as an offering to your smile
And held tight as we rode the flying fox from the highest
Landing of my fear
And rather than choose separation I joined with you again
Each time rising one step
Until binoculars in hand and resting on the bonnet of our car
I watched you run down steps and through the dune grass
Into the surf
You picked up kelp waved and yelled
"Look its mermaid's hair.........Come in for a swim"
And me lying back in all trust your one arm under my head
And the other my shoulders
When like a priestess lowering me into your waters you
Baptised me
And then I saw in the waves an eerie sea
Where lashes flow to eyes clinging to a raft
In waters never seen before
And now as I watch you sleep on the beach
With your hair spread against a pillow of sand
I am entrusted with all that is
Nose lips mouth and brow cradled in the clouds
Woman on the other side shoulders in white sheets
I run my fingers through your hair as you sleep

I Am Not That

Not the worker
Not the father
Not the dreamer
Not the peacemaker
Not the mapmaker
Not planter of poles lines in the drift of mystery
Not holder of questions like coins of celestial currency
Nor holder of amulet in the hands of pilgrim or desert father
Perhaps I am of the web strung between gate posts
In parkland where the moon seals the night

Calvary

1

The Calvary is settled on a hill
And from a windowed portico
I overlook the practice field of golfers
Towards Adelaide

2

A backfill of buildings
Where white sails
Grandstand the Adelaide oval
Against the Royal Adelaide Hospital
And surround of Research Centre

All on a day when clouds threaten
But vision is clear through the parklands
Into city streets
Where the tumult of parade extends
From King William to Pulteney Street

3

In Rundle Mall there are those who trumpet faith
And those with faces stewed in sour juices
There are groups of schoolchildren
At one end boys strong chested
With arms carrying
The litter of their daydreams
At the other end girls
Uniformed from skirt to crown

In the swirl between buskers
And vendors
Bent-shouldered elders
Carry invisible sacks of their day

4

I watch from Calvary
Where drops and half-drops
Of existence are carried
Along a tube transfusing
Blood to a patient

5

At first glance from above
The North Parklands
The fairways and greens
Wear the same uniform

But beyond projection
Trees hold spears and grapple
With clouds in the shape of snakes

A gum holds the head
Of a snake
While another thrusts
A spear

Round and round cloud coils
Solidifying scales and head
To take each blow

6

I turn to the woman visiting
Her daughter in the next bed
But instead of talk of cloud and snake and war
Words are said for the poor girl
With plaits laid out on sheets

7

Grandmother holds hands as one fist
Elbows out she chants
Why
Why
   Oh why this little girl
A father bent at the edge of the bed

8

I see the battle with the snakes
I see those here
Who bear their own crosses
In between I shake
Where else to wait it out
For the angels
Who guide the sick and weak

9

Is this world
A mere rustle in the long grass
Of my dreams
Or the creak of floorboards

10

I have heard the stories of the trees
The great battles
Between them and the shadows
For what nourishes
And as I look again towards the streets of Adelaide
Where in the Mall a woman sits with child
As flowers are sold
I wonder if tree angel or shadow will prevail

11

There is beauty and desire in these streets
Whether wrapped in spring or autumn leaves
The Art Gallery is full of myth and imagery
To morph and weave into manicured belief

12

Again I turn to the young girl lying in the bed
Mother's hands cup the child's head
A young man just beyond the bed
Steadied

13

There are so many statues pedestalled in this city
If only a few could get up
And walk up Montefiore Hill
To the steps of this place
And tell me what is wrong with this little girl
I know there is childhood and there is family
I know there are gardens where children play
I am not so foolish to believe all is good in between

14

There is war and death and disease
There is reward and there is betrayal
I see the battle for this child

This girl with plaits
I wonder if she too sees the trees
And cloud and knows the path through

This is no dream where I am a knight
Guiding a child through a maze
But if I could sing the lines
To give her journey a chance I would

15

For some the lines are traded
With the priest at the altar
For others the lines are sung
Around the fire by elders
But for the anointed
The lines are heaven sent

16

I have heard it said the battle is only won
When you find the secret name of the god
Worshipped by the enemy
Maybe this is where the answer lies

17

So is it in the clouds or in the saint's eyes
Where truth lies

Today I have a passion for naming the shadows
A bush-ranger cunning
To snare these images of life and death and all between
I have them here in the grass
Bound
Through their pockets
And possessions I browse
Some cringe
Some defiant
But cowering inside
Some shamed
Some angered and threatening to kill
But each will confess
Their name
They will

18

They threaten to revolt
But I will find what will make the little girl wake
And walk with me in the sunny streets
I do not want to see this girl carried in procession
Down the aisle
Where all will say
She was dressed in white and pure
So innocent
She could have ridden the swan
In the lily pond of belief

19

I see cloud filter
Through window to her sheets

Light fingers inspecting a treat
Stroking her hair
While those around are oblivious
Trapped in their own thoughts
Of funeral casket and memorial

20

It is then I am of the tree
And bite right through
The body of this snake
And in the recoil to the parklands
I see jettisoned in its wake
The kiss of a young woman
Against the lips of a lover
Cloistered in stained glass and bay window
And then brown hair worn in the bun
Of marriage and children
Followed by image
Straight-nosed in belief
The last as if framed in a locket
Blue-eyed and hair parted

21

I see the kernel of what nourishes
The ribboned glow
Of images stream back
Halo around the little girl
And re-enter leaving a slight tail
Before all is enveloped
Into her body

22

I am beyond these folk
Oblivious still to my presence
Beyond all they have inherited
And the generations woven
Into their prejudices
Beyond finger-pointing
And whispers at the dinner table

23

I look into parklands
A fixed and stony stare
A honed meditative trance
Beyond the topiary of ideas
To where trees shiver
Where fairways are robed
In a cool green which overflows
And pours from the basin of trees
Which cluster and column
Along the fairway

24

I stand against the shadows
Which circle within the walls
Of belief
Step beyond tree and snake
Beyond reflection
And stoic laziness of defiance
Beyond all avatar
And stare

25

I am not naked
I am the wrap of green
Liquid and light
The float and stretch
From fingertips to toes
Of all that is was and will be

26

I call back to hospital window
For those inside to jump in
But my words are never heard
By those with questions to solve

27

The green quenches
And the little girl
Is now a woman by the stream
Flowers in her hair and lilies on her knees
I call out to her
But still I cannot be heard
As she is on a different path
And there are others by the banks
Playing sport
Picking flowers
And dancing

28

I cannot be heard
As I am between here and there
In the gleam of a dream

Aware of love and death and war
Aware of snake and cloud
But somehow in between
In that seam of internal light
Which runs down fairways
And putts on the greens
While in the city below
Men and women
Pick leaves from the flowers
Of their own workload
Kiss in rooms
Drink in bars to ease the pain

29

I return and join the fight for liberty
In time before rainbow and hills
In the round of clouds and snakes
I swear I will name you

30

In the fight the shape of a hand
And form of a shoulder
Determined to take me as a prize

I name you
I name you
I name you
I shout
For you are my pride
My inauthenticity
My avoidance

My Doubt
Dragging me to its lair

31
The little girl I have worried about
Has risen from her bed
We stand face to face
The beast gone
A ball of yarn at my feet
And with hands outstretched
We thread yarn between our hands
Stretching and shaping at will

32
Once again the bubble of the streets
Scaffolds the landscape of Adelaide
And the fairways and trees
Again pattern parklands
Bordered by window frame

In the Letting Go

In the letting go and emptying of the lived world
There is the suspension which bridges between
Caterpillar and butterfly and unfurls what always was
Into the wings of the Monarch

Bill

At dusk we build a fire and sit...
Bill a contractor who builds roads into mystery
Leans against his grader
Looks into silence and says...
Have you ever visited the Underside of Bark
The Underside of Bark where parquetry of thought
Gives way to water ways and squid and fish swim in the deep
While stingray sleep
Where crabs click their claws and whales glide watery streets

As above through the green where the oars of others ply
Fish as many as the stars are ornamental ribbons of tinsel
Locked in schools
Why not depart and join the turtle in caravan on this reef

2

Sometimes I just need another perspective
As I learn the way to converse with who I want to be
In nation building the one after regeneration
After the tide has washed the course away
Or fire storm has ravaged the bush
In a new form I might see from above
Crops which wallpaper Kununurra
Green panels against the earth
Lightly soiled where undergrowth has taken hold

In this perspective I could at once
Scour the grit from dry lake beds
Follow ancient trading routes
From Parachilna to the Gulf of Carpentaria

Rub my chest against the Gammon Ranges
Snake my way along lines sung by others
See the fist-hold of red dirt is not as tight as imagined
And that dead lakes pool and die towards some greater cause

3

All seems patch quilt and blanket from above
Some sleeping soul moves below
Every now and then a bump or two rises as an island
Here I am closer in the search for waterholes

Ripped from my boat the primordial reptilian beast
Of stunted growth which lurks in the deepest of sinkholes
Of the soul takes me in a death roll

A new life and a step closer the water is of Chinese tea
Lukewarm by the time I have taken a sip
Where an assortment of fish dart pivot
And posture not to be seen

Here I am the green turtle of the Kennedy River
In this water my shell is polished armour
My head tilted towards the star drops
Which muster on the water line
Little cities of light float in this place

I am the stems of water lilies riding above pads
Purple leaves interleaved and spread
In the shape of a woman
Arms and legs outstretched
Buoyant in this swimming place

Head back and eyes beyond fern and cliff
Beyond the source of waterfall

4

I'm either this
Or an empty stubby of four X
Pissed in and dumped by the main gate at the races

5

From Innamincka to Roxby punters travel for miles
To play the odds and bet Darwin Sydney Hobart
Melbourne and Adelaide at the same time
And when others have gone I'm just
One of the discarded and disfigured betting stubs
Swept by broom as the bookie quenches thirst
In the VIP room

6

It doesn't matter how many museums I might visit
Or dogs I carry in my Ute
It doesn't matter how many bare-chested fights
I've been in
The crowd is always going to gather
There is always someone who will want to take me on

Round one they might call me the Duke of Earl
Punching above my weight

Round two I'm sitting in a chair
Trying to stop the bleeding
By round three my opponent is named the Savage
And I'm gone

In that half-dead state I see that I'm only part
Of a side show of some travelling circus
About me are those happy who by my beating
Have cleansed themselves until next time

7

Instead I take the journey to where land
Blends with sea
Where orange vines thread the sand
Like discarded fishing nets
Where little flowers are butterflies
With tips of toes glued to sand
And pink-flowered wings
Which parachute in the wind

8

All around water bubbles and brims
On the Gulf spiderwebs are spinnakers in the breeze
Cockles litter the shore and seagrass grows in clumps
Spinifex clusters

All this against water which froths corrugates
Murmurs and fills in the cracks

9

In its unspoilt form
The sand mirrors the lapping of the tide
Which impresses the seal of ocean onto beach

Everything from fine drawn lines
At the water's edge

To patterned slivers of sand
Is bejewelled with pebble
Shell and pleated blue
Golden are the steps to this beach

10

In this world if I'm not a gull
Picking through the shore
Or floating on a board waiting for the surf
I'm a Pilchard head severed from the rest
Strung to a hook by a rubber band

On the end of a rod above my head
My closest moon is the sinker
As with bowl of the arm I'm in the blue
In for the ride but deaf and blind

11

I might take photographs of dolphins
While standing knee deep in water
Count the gulls or fish off the reef
Swing by the coast or settle on a shack
But while I seek to farm what I can
From this land
Bill pulls his grader to a halt
The taste of sugarcane in his mouth

Far from where six singlets hang from a line
Past where bitumen turns to dust
He steps from the cab and crosses the silver blade
Wipes his arm across the blue of his singlet

And looks at the Dingo fence which marks this stop
Fence wire intent as law runs left and right
A bearded dragon with puffed up chest cranes
Towards the sun

In the distance dirt lifts and twists
In a wurlie wurlie

Bill pinches his Adam's Apple
And clears his throat
Climbs back into his grader
Sites the blade against rock and undergrowth
And pushes towards Coober Pedy

12

As we rake north from the verge where a bearded dragon
With scales from hind legs to face stands as a gatekeeper
The tread of tyre draws a corrugated script

Here where bitumen trailed into red dirt some kilometres back
The road kill includes blown out tyres frayed grit and oil
Encrusted off casts

Here on a good day Sturt Desert Peas black faced and
red winged meet in committee on high stalks
Feeders strung with fingernails of leaves every so often kissed
By dew which pouts in a bed of green leaf and counterweights
The regeneration within this matted relief

On other days Turkey Bush marks the way
Not the sort which flocks like bottlebrush or wattle

But that which propels in the wind with fine slender purple
Blades which are blood red where they thread into rosemary
Stem and lift in the heat

13

Back at Maree a dog with legs pressed on the bonnet of a wreck
Stares up the road for his master while an albino kangaroo
And brolga pick through short grass in a dusty paddock

There is discarded muffler stripped tyre and broken crab claw
In the tufts and mounds of this place where wire
Is strung between jarrah posts and washing stiffens in the sun
Where before he left Bill loaded his grader
Packed with pick shovel and spirit level and then threw in an
Esky and his swag
Poured a coffee and then sat under a flaking bullnose veranda
Reading the maps in the clouds and looking to those greater
Roads

14

Eventually Bill and I will drive past paddocks
Where hay is stacked in bales in panoramic shot headstones
Tilted left and right and bearing inscription in thread of gold
We will drive where rain in the distance tumbles and coils
Then through places where the rear vision mirror is fried
Reflecting spite in the sun

This trip will open fissures in tyres and chip windscreens
Burst gaskets on pumps and snap couplings on exhausts
Crack radiators and rip open tarps

15

Where I am now and where I want to be are platforms
At outback towns dotted along the railways of the mind
But railway towns sometimes die and memory passes them by
When their patrons find ways to venture past terminus
And deeper into the interior

16

There will be no petrol for 500 kms
The unsealed road is impassable when wet
And beware the buffalo in the middle of the road
Or country killed meat will be barbequed on the campfire
But dine in or takeaway
There is no excuse
Not to set out
Where I am going
There's no grog
No guns
No weapons
No drunks

17

Only the stewards are allowed on this level clipboards in hand
But I forget the steward's report and just grab a saddle
And head for the stalls

The rest huddle in their associations or tiptoe on unsound
Ground at the quarry's edge from which are cut the building
Blocks of the words used to build their monuments

Some will get encouragement and some will get their name
On a board with inscription and all
But it's what happens when you're on the rodeo ride that counts

Hold on tight and roll to the side
It's all in the eye of the stirrup
When to push and when not
Even a kid has to learn to take the knocks
Go in arms crossed but learn to rise

Some come out with the rest
As they gather and walk to the bar tent
Others will be quenched by the wonder
Of what lies across Bill's desert

18

In this land there are hulks left to rust
Only their states of decomposition vary
My lot might be that of an old tractor
Wandering dying stock
The reliable weathered fence post
I might be the pair of old boots
Where spider webs now froth
The tap on the tanker rusted shut
A broken chair in a desert drive-in theatre

19

From Ceduna to Maree
Cemeteries bank those anchored
To their indispensable lives
Through silence and mystery

Methodist Catholic Seventh Day Adventist
Anglican United Ununited
Orthodox Unorthodox
Jew Muslim Hindu Buddhist
Indigenous
Non Indigenous
The Lot
Invited Uninvited
Buried or cremated
Marked and unmarked
Some sites in the shape of trundle beds
Some with their own fences
Like children's cots
Some piles of rock
Or burnt out-car wrecks
Others open books
Their neighbour's dark pits
Bordered by necklaces of little stones
All rust and grist chaff and bone
Strained back through dirt and undergrowth
Where desert mice sleep in shallow burrows
Then raise as dingoes howl back and forth
Their rights through the night

20

In this land there is process and being where senses
Are road kill to the expanse of silence and mystery
And waterholes are a rare jewel
But what sustains against all which consumes and exhausts

What quenches thirst and permits you to converse
Where otherwise nothing is said is the ineffable mouthful of
Light

21

I peel up the roof sheets
Find the barrels to store all possible
Drop my shorts in the desert
Leave them to become caked in sand
Home for lizards and mice

Skin might be peppered with rivets
Boarded with timber threaded by wire
Tattooed rusted and flaked
But I pry the windows from their frames
Abandon this homestead and cross the bridge
Scale the old corrugated fence
Leave the motorbike to rust in the sand
Pour from the broken bore pipe
Forget the beams which span
Between silos of knowledge
Jump like the kangaroo
Past old ground and in renewal
Leave ironing board and moth-eaten sofa behind
What is left is a pile of railroad tracks rusting in the sun

22

If we get out as far Birdsville or Cameron Corner
Where camel and cow have perished and water tanks
Are bullet ridden and shotgunned by wind and sand
While galahs perch on windmills safe by the bore

And ants build their mounds as this earth coughs dust
I'll be sure to stand at the border with feet in two different
States

23

Today pinnacles are decaying jagged teeth
And life resembles dry tree roots
But it is Bill's footprint in the sand that counts
By the lizard tracks
Through corrugated dune
The only green bush in this place
So I muster those forty-four gallon drums
Rusty lipped and barnacled
Long ring-barked
Aqua blue undercoat baked in the sun
The peeling flaking skin of melanoma peppered vessels
Worn as sandpaper and dragged across the deep
Where bottom feeders reek

Roll them up one by one
The Super the Ultra the Unleaded
Stack the Jet Fuel the Av Gas
The Formula Diesel
All highly flammable
Snapshot them sideways
Piled one on top another
Interlocking rods totem high
200 litres upon 200 litres
Of the vulnerable exposed
Out here in Bill's desert
Stacked packed and racked

Take the lids of these barrels as coins
But the real money is in sorting the batches
The filled from the half filled
The important barrels are the ones which will float
When the big wet comes and lake beds rise
There is art in the welding together of the craft by which
To Navigate watershed from one side to the next
But there is being in learning to speak with the currents
And waterways mapped by the saints

24

Jigsaw puzzled tufts of dry lake bed wheeze in clay pans from
Alice Springs to Innamincka and we need to be sure of the
Underfoot as we cross the lonely desolate beautiful and tranquil
Where drought-ridden lakebeds bare the skeletons of cows
And sheep in a tight fist

25

Great expanses of time and place where tiled alfresco
Under the blue seeds the occasional husk of being
As the smallest crevice leaves room for salt bush to rise
In the salt pans of Lake Eyre where rendered blue salt mound
Turns pale and mummifies past lives in ghostly white crystal
Shrouds

26

In the flowering in Bill's Desert there is the perennial tongue
Spoken in the deepest contemplation of the unknowing to turtle
And bearded dragon

But there is also the cruelty of pilgrimage to the threshold
Where unable to hold onto love fragile as a shed leaf and crisp
With disbelief there is no waterhole to quench thirst
There is the fall back into the clothing of appointments
Charts and words which shackle mind and cloud
Which grind through grass branch and rootstock
Reducing all to church office and monuments
Cruel is the insight of the lover who cannot hold onto love

27

As ochre washes from horizon Bill with an initiated eye picks
The ruby fruit from salt bush and soaks a handful in water to
Brew a sweet tea
He then takes the leaves of this bush crushes and wraps them in
Cloth applying a poultice to a sunburnt arm as dust rises
Then falls into the earth as if into a cavern then springs up again
As Bill nods in silent conversation
Bill strips his singlet and stands with bare chest
As the truth of him empties into the Underside of Bark.

The Gift

Ever hear of a place called Stawell
Were the first words Jack ever said to me
Jack lived for the day when one of his own would win
The Gift and wear the sash which marks a life

I have walked through grass which combs the backside
Of crushed stone to the line where the path lapses
And eucalyptus oil trickles from muscle
Into recesses surveyed and pegged into lanes
Set side by side for the flight of six finalists who stand
Their ground as pretenders are culled

Tectonic plates squeeze breath from continents
This Easter Monday as I stand at one hundred
And twenty metres of damp rolled grass
The distance between who I am
And who I want to be
Green thought perforated
By the steel talons of the sprinter's spikes
Shoulders stiffen at the whistle's sharp call to the blocks

Let the blocks be your friend
Push Push Push
Get a Good start
Pre-empt the gun
Fast Fast Fast

The unanswered question settles on the afternoon tide
Panther tiger leopard lion slide into the chamber

Of the starter's gun
Bullets of flesh poised in the tension
Between trigger and thumb
Flags flap in the wind
Bibs red white pink blue black and green
Are strapped tight as punters swirl like barley
In the betting ring and heads crane ten deep from terraces

I am the black smoke chased by the recoil of thunder
As the race begins
Ten to twenty metres
Stride upon stride
The measure of bookies odds
The stopwatch's squinted eye
Twenty to thirty metres
I am the glare between shadow
Thirty to forty metres
I am the stitching of bib shorts
Shoes undone
Forty to fifty metres
I am space and time clinging to marrow
Fifty to sixty metres
I am pure light

Come on Move it
The vein in Jack's forehead rises
This run will make you strong
Remember
If you're not with me
Then you're against me
If you're not on my team

Then get out
It's that easy
Are you on my team
Are you on my team

Sixty to seventy metres
I am in that field
Where no name is written on the sash
Seventy to eighty metres
I am hammer chisel
And rock face
Between start line and finish gate
Eighty to ninety metres
The scent of my ancestors
And offspring permeates this place
Ninety to one hundred metres
This lane shakes

One hundred to one hundred and ten metres
I am the roar
Of re-entry as meteor burns in the atmosphere of the opaque

One hundred and ten metres to one hundred and twenty
I lunge at the line with chest outstretched
I break the tape and my stable mates jump the fence

As friends and paparazzi swell the crowd around me
I am hoisted above shoulders like an offering to the gods
Raised on a platform of hands arms and words
Then with a thud I hit the ground
The future moves like a swarm of bees to another hive

One hundredth of a second is the difference as the blue sash
Marks another life

Leaving the words
Ever hear of a place called Stawell
To twist in the wind as I look to the ground

And so I have fronted the line
And wrapped my hand around the neck
Of space and time
Peeled away tectonic plates
Where erosion meets being
And grass combs the backside of crushed stone

Ceres[1]

Granite bed in a ward halfway up a hill
Where deep blades of grass sash
Headstones left and right
And rosemary eats the sun
Where gulls glide in wide arcs
And the running of the surf
From Front Beach
Through sea grass and dune
Spills from coastal track
In a gentle hush

In the wash all folds
Into fingers of surf
From Back Beach
And kneads the body
Of this peninsula
Where Bass Strait
Presses against bay

Rockpools dot water's edge
Where little creatures live and die
In seasons compressed
Into the rise and fall of the tide

---

1. **Ceres** was the name given by the athletics coach Percy Wells Cerutty to his home in Portsea where he trained athletes including Herb Elliott who won the Gold Medal for the 1,500 metres at the 1960 Rome Olympic Games in a then world record time.

The wind tongues into sandhill
Feathered by dune grass
Draws back in a dry scrape
To the now incessant slap
Of wave against shore

They say for us there is no
Thread of soul in this land
Which swallows lame and fit whole
Yet why take the pilgrimage
Trace steps through dune
Four hundred metres from surf club
Where young Elliott had surged up sand hill
Towards Olympic Dream

Knees lift and arms pump
Through dune
With the repetition of incoming tide
As Percy preaches virtues
Of stoic and Spartan life

Two bound in time
You ran the beach
From Portsea to Sorrento
Each footprint a sinkhole
As you shuttled
Between waterline and shore
Not threatened by tentacle
Of outgoing tide

We too have run upon this earth
Building homes along the coast
Bitumen suits now worn by tracks
Down to car parks and beach
Where showers wash sand from toes
Forming fresh puddles in worn hollows

More than a weatherboard house
Or the frame of your grave
The hands of this place
Sprinkle salt and wind into being
Each blade of sea grass
Is each step taken
Each to be taken
On the pilgrim's trail

I sing this song of Ceres
Lighthouse to being
Beacon to insignificance
As I rest on the path
And listen to breath and step
Through seagrass and dune

Round the bluff they come
In single file
Percy tucked behind Elliott's stride
The thread of their camber
From Portsea to Sorrento
Perth and beyond

Thread followed to the coil
From last bus stop
Along unsealed track
To fly wire door
And the question
Is there room for one more?

Shells

1

Water clears
Tide rakes seaweed
Magnifies feet

2

Horizon is a picked peach
As water laps at my hips
My chest
My chin
Until sandbank and plateau
Give way to undertow

3

And the question
Do I swim across the rip
Or let the flow
Take me out

4

The test of authenticity
Of resilience and constitution
Begins as cramp seizes legs
And waves batter head

5

In the rip is said
Of shell and pearl
And salt and wind

The Shaman's eye
Planted within

6

Fertilised in an apron of surf
And the flaying of feet
I am hauled from beach
And holiday home
Tumble and turn
With salt and shell
Sandpapered by the wind

7

In the time between breaths
Where all is summersault
And fingers rake for ladder
I catch a shell and then another

8

I hold a shell against my flesh
One side an ear
That listens to my whispered talk
The other a heel
Of dry skin
Partly compressed in chalk white
With patches of rough granite

Part heel upon this world
Part ear to my words
Exhibit one

Of a coroner's report
Of an incident off a beach

9

The second exhibit
Held to the light
Holds terraces from dimple of chin
To toothless mouth
With back molars intact

And on the face more terraces
This time holding beaches and dunes
Calcified white
This one contours my face
Like a mask

10

Through mouth towards the light
I see in the skull
Where forehead should have been
The cornea of an eye
Staring from the sky

All else is vaulted ceiling
Of an impressive building
Beyond which is caught
In a net of glass
A swirl of mist and cloud
Fossilised into the core
Of the frontal lobe

11

In these waters
I meet fingertips
Arm and body
All of shell

On my back
With shells
Supporting my neck
I look towards peaks
Of cloud which summit
Through horizon
To the other side

12

The next is like waterline
Where sea reclines
Pretty as a hand-held fan
Fluttering wafer thin
Density of skin
Underside an amphitheatre
Funnelling a current
Rough as pumice stone
Through ear canal

13

In the swirl of the deep
A shell is a skullcap
Here bits and pieces of mind
Are barnacled to the underside
Where fingers rake

And brush to read the braille
From snowcapped peaks
Which range left and right

14

Unpacked those small as bone
Ancient in their wear
With peaks and troughs
Of range stamped with moon
And caves robed in white
Where paintings wait to be read
To those like a bit of grit
Face and name washed flat
Ridged and grooved
Driftwood in the universe

15

In the deep
All is foetus
All is glow
And each shell sings
Of shell and pearl and salt and wind
The Shaman's eye planted within

16

There is moon
There is swirl
Where back of shell
Is the ridge
Of a humpback whale

17

As waves agitate
And arms and legs stall
Each shell an outcrop
Where little tents dot slopes
And little fires glow
Like stars

18

Here is one
A nomad's tent
It crawls and hovers
At any chance

19

By another a potter presses
Work between hands
Clasped in prayer

20

Shell is entrance to a cave
Where light frames a woman
With flint and spark
In her eyes

21

Two sides of a shell
Clasp in prayer
One side is pitted by bullet hole and axe
The other side bears scars
In the shape of anchors
And the lash

22

I prise open a clam
And inspect the womb
One side a resting place
The other a pool
In which I snorkel
Off the south coast

23

I name each fish
As they pass in schools
Which meander
Through glint of sunlight
In ruffled water

24

Each knuckled part
By each knuckled part
A fragment of shell
To give a name to each
Is to give face

25

The name for face
Old as time
But the eye
Must be where I lie
No matter which shell
Sits on my desk

26

Here the form of a head
With granite mane
Flowing down shoulders
To legs

27

Cave wall
Neolithic painting
Of fish
Spears arrows
And wild beast
Of mantra ray
Through the deep

28

Whether seashell
Is kneecap or joint
Knife for gutting
Or a sacrificial piece
On each lip
I take the offering
With respect

29

This shell
I name manta ray
It sidles to my lips
And I take communion
From this piece

30

This one speaks
Of a rip in the tide
Of shell and pearl
And salt and wind
Of the Shaman's eye

One side a flipper
The other secretes
A pearl lacquer
And where they meet
I feed on nectar

31

In embryonic nectar
The slow glide from knee to calf
The accession through rib
To settle on Breastplate

32

First they rise as filigree
Then turn hard dark
As coffin lid

Encased in shell and debris
All is mollusc inside
I suck for air
Under capsized shell
Which sits cleanly
On my mouth

This piece breathes
As I breathe
Heaves as I heave

What keeps me alive
Saves my soul
Are tiny holes
I spot from within
First one then more
Appear in the stratosphere

33

My shells move with a groan
First the one against my nose
The scent of salt in the air
Then my shoulders
Roll left and right

34

The first begins to crystallise
Wraps around my big toe
The tear of pearl a third eye
Then slowly clears
Into crystal form

35

Clamped by thumb and finger
There is a prying and a slit
Just deep enough to pry away the skin
Then the burrowing underneath

Tailored to my form this shell
Cups my toes and balls of feet

36
Another tunnels like the wind
Under my skin
Although small somehow spreads
A power from head to toe

The back of each calf
A resting place
Deep in muscle where capillary
Like ivy webs each shell
To its spot

37
Knees are mirrored
In that each receives
Crystallised like an eye
A pearled shell
One a receiver
The other a responder

38
I can twist and contort
So one knee presses against
What I think is my ear
And one knee against
Where my mouth should be

39

Here I pause
Indifferent to other shells
Which burrow from hip to chest

Here I float as a navigator
Waiting to report
The cartography of the deepest
Ravine

40

Now the shell in one hand
Is an ear
And the shell in the other
Is a mouth

I am both mouth and ear
The mouth a swirl of cloud
The ear ridged and compact

41

My hips ache
As great force is used
To embed each shell
The first a dry bed lake
Cracked and fractured
Scrapping my inside

42

Salt and dust
Harbours in cities

Under each dry flake
Peppers and dusts
The shell which sits as mouth plate

43
Another wants the marrow
From my bones
It slits me from thigh to hip
And in one great rip
Cuts through to bone
Then settles as crumpled sheet

44
The next is where my cock
Should be
Hangs like a loin cloth
Just under my skin

My belly hangs
Where shell scoops
Through my digestive tract

Breast plate holds an older form
This one placed by fingers
With precision and care

45
Fingers press shells under my skin
My hands and arms are furrowed
Shells sit where joints have been
An Adam's apple of a shell
Sits in my throat

46

I am cobbled together
A man of shells
Complete with parasites
Little creatures
Which dandruff the nooks
And crannies
Of my shelves

47

Mouth eyes and nose spin
Massive blades
Helicopter from my side
A ladder of shells in the form
Of a dangling man
Rises then recoils

48

I float in this place
The sea a gentle rush
The water so clear
I can see right through me
To insemination
To shells which dot seabed
Just within a plunge's reach

A billion ridges and groves mark
The story of this place
Of stars and caves and water waves

49

I float with eyes to the shore
Where time has banked like sand
Against dune grass
Where a track to a beach
Is an estuary of thought
Bordered by low shrub and grass

50

And with the roll of a seal
I ply to the shore
And to a salamander
Tinkering and clacking rebirth
As the surf sings
Of shell and pearl and salt and wind
The Shaman's eye planted within

I Chased Him

I chased him through the streets of Adelaide
Through the parklands and beyond
Set a snare in undergrowth
The other side of Gepps Cross
Then cast a line out to Taree
Traced along the Gammon Rangers
Held Wilpena Pound as a trophy on my walls
Tracked through shrouds of desert sand
Swung back towards the coast
Reached into rockpools along the shore
Returned to streetscape
Peeled letters from flaking signs
And listened to the tap tap tap from darkened alleyways
Thought that I would be led by angels through the gateway
Then hand against gum I looked to read the bark
The face of Warrior Shaman Centurion Seer
Coiled around the fallacy of name and place
I chased him into the underside
Where stingray and turtle caravan
I swam in deep blue waters
Then made my salamander walk to the shore
Waterholes now not so far between

Breath

Breath from greater breath dissipates
Into providence shaped by mastery to move
Mountains stars and lifetimes about
Like flakes dished and panned from one side
Of a celestial riverbank to the other
By a prospector sustained by flecks
Which pass from one side to the next

Pebble

Marbled in swirls to the centre
The cloth unwrapped was bigger than the sea
As the hand of me plunged deep
Into the mystery of how a pebble came to be

My Run

There is a place where a gumtree stands
And holds bark in the shape of a face
A face I have claimed and named as mine
A mouth and eyes millennia old
Which watch from a clearing
Where a creek flows under a small bridge
From where I began my run
I stretch against the railing and wait
For others to finish
The creek today is steady and flows
From the undergrowth
Cascades and runs as if pursued
Under the bridge
I try to trace from where the water came
But the flow is lost in a crowd
Of shrub grass and trees
In the time I am here a boy sets off for a run
Then a couple pass by
As I look to the creek an old woman returns
One leg now on railing I stretch my hamstring
Lean with shoulders rounded as the grass
On each of the banks which crest towards the centre as a crown
And while I stretch one by one the little drops of dew which
Have clung to the railing break from their seal
And join the run of water to the other side
I say to you to paint this creek in the time I have would be an
Achievement

Beyond

Having withstood the arrows of the wordless
And made peace with the shadows
Emancipated from chains of the archival
My wish is to be scattered
Each breath each step each piece
Eyes nails and toes
Not held by a vessel or coveted as a relic
But cast into silence
Beyond ransom or sovereign

Between Chapters

What belief presses a leaf between chapters
So that in time all becomes wafer thin copperplate
Embossed with dry lines where veins had been
What power then draws another to this book
To seed new growth where dust has settled
What gift the breath to cleanse and regenerate
To turn the arid into cool cotton sheets
Which hold words stirring in sleep
What wakes as green stem held to the light

Suit of Anonymity

And once again wrapped in the fur and cloth
Of dream when the moon can be mistaken for the sun
And mist runs like a river under a bridge
Where creatures graze on banks
Light springs like a tiger
And part of me darts from the grass
To again wear the suit of anonymity

Cormorant

The thrust from blocks cast of air
The plunge of feather and talon
The arrowhead dive of avarice
Into the gift of rebirth
Then the snap and flick
To bring one life to a stop
And in the sacrifice lies the exchange
Where feigned death is washed
From wilted eyes as one heartbeat lost
Feeds another in the chase

Ground Cover

Green-stemmed ground cover
In a mediative hold
Presses against weeds of imperfection

As a beetle circles over and over
The same head of lettuce
Like a lawyer reading the constitution

And Bell Peppers ring and Peaches sing
Of the time the path was softened
By the blossom of what could be

I Am

As steps which drop like light rain
Pearl and tear along a windowpane
Then huddle before watershed
Unnamed in my tribute to the perpetual

The First Wish

To see what lives in that moment when the sun
Breaks over crest and spills into deepest sight
Laying bare all manner of shadow cast from the dye
Of the ineffable

The Second Wish

To read in the scrabble the script
Each time as fresh and crisp as the first

The Third Wish

Torn between the gift and thirst
I fill my glass and wait

Garland

Perennial the crown woven of barbed wire
Fence post dune grass leaf and shell